Creating Floral Centerpieces

Bill Murphy, AIFD

Schiffer Publishing Ltd
4880 Lower Valley Road, Atglen, Pennsylvania 19310

Acknowledgements

I would like to thank Tina Skinner at Schiffer Publishing, Ltd. for photography and editorial assistance. I also offer special thanks to student shadow, Sterling Arjona.

Dedication

To my three kids,
Alixandria, Brandon, and Gabriella,
the most amazing, talented individuals I know.
This is a tribute to the joy you bring to my life.

Other Schiffer Books By The Author:

Entertaining With Flowers: The Floral Artistry of Bill Murphy, 0-7643-2556-6, $29.95

Bridal Flowers: Bouquets, Boutonniéres, Corsages, 978-0-7643-3485-6, $24.99

Other Schiffer Books on Related Subjects:

The Bridal Bouquet Book, 0-7643-2197-8, $39.95

Copyright ©2010 by Bill Murphy and Schiffer Publishing, Ltd.
Library of Congress Control Number: 2010923336

Designed by Stephanie Daugherty
Type set in Snell Blk BT/Snell BT/Zurich BT

ISBN: 978-0-7643-3459-7
Printed in China

Schiffer Books are available at special discounts for bulk purchases for sales promotions or premiums. Special editions, including personalized covers, corporate imprints, and excerpts can be created in large quantities for special needs. For more information contact the publisher:

Published by Schiffer Publishing Ltd.
4880 Lower Valley Road
Atglen, PA 19310
Phone: (610) 593-1777; Fax: (610) 593-2002
E-mail: Info@schifferbooks.com

For the largest selection of fine reference books on this and related subjects, please visit our web site at
www.schifferbooks.com
We are always looking for people to write books on new and related subjects. If you have an idea for a book please contact us at the above address.

This book may be purchased from the publisher.
Include $5.00 for shipping.
Please try your bookstore first.
You may write for a free catalog.

In Europe, Schiffer books are distributed by
Bushwood Books
6 Marksbury Ave.
Kew Gardens
Surrey TW9 4JF England
Phone: 44 (0) 20 8392 8585; Fax: 44 (0) 20 8392 9876
E-mail: info@bushwoodbooks.co.uk
Website: www.bushwoodbooks.co.uk

Table of Contents

Introduction

Would you have a wedding cake without icing? Why have a dinner party without beautiful flowers?

Flowers are one way you can express your personality when you host a party. You can keep it very simple or you can create a grand centerpiece that takes everybody's breath away. So, if you are a bad cook, the least you can do is offer your guests something nice to look at.

When you go to a dinner party, what two things do you remember? The food, if it was good or bad, and the way the dinner table looked. It is easy to forget everything else, especially if there was wine.

When creating a look for someone I take a look at their house or the location where the event is going to be, talk to them about what they like, and find out what the event is for. Is it a wedding, an anniversary, or a shower? Then I design from there.

In the course of creating this book, I have attempted to scale the projects with a modest budget in mind. My greatest joy, however, is creating the truly spectacular. I love to add more, and then some more. Some of my past creations include a tower of pineapples and grasses that mimicked a palm tree and stood about as tall, a gigantic glass vase with 300 orchids cascading out of it, and a fifteen-foot tall floral display for a buffet table (the table was only four feet wide and they had to have room for the food!).

My most memorable pieces, however, have been for weddings. I take a lot of time with each couple because I know that what I am doing is making a statement at the start of their new life together. Many times I will use family heirlooms for the vases and containers, especially if the vessel is from a family member who has passed. These pieces represent the loved ones who are unable to attend.

Whenever I do a function, clients tell me it is the most memorable event in their lives. I think this is because I put a piece of myself, and the client into my work—it is very personal for both of us. Because of this every single piece I do is a one of a kind. You will never see two of my events look the same. They are all totally customized for the person hosting the event.

I hope that by learning some of my basic techniques, you too will be able to develop your own style and embellish your events with your own personality.

Basic Presentations

oday, wire is the preferred tool and accessory of any self-respecting florist, followed closely by faux gems. Equally important is floral glue, which allows you to affix flower heads and leaves to virtually any surface while keeping them fresh for hours. After that, your imagination is the limit.

I have tried to present a variety of ideas, from pieces with shiny eye-catchers to those with warm tones and textures that awe with the beauty of nature to arrangements that evoke nostalgia or help establish a theme for your event or holiday. The goal, however, is to review basic skills and apply them to creations that will satisfy your urge to create and impress your friends and family. Stock up on some florist wire, floral foam, and floral glue, then search your top shelves for interesting vessels.

Note: Many of the supplies used throughout these presentations come from Oasis Floral Products in Kent, Ohio. For more information, please contact 1-800-321-8286 or http://sona.oasisfloral.com.

Hand Tying a Bouquet

The first skill any florist needs is the ability to tie a basic bouquet. Instead of practicing with flowers, try working with two-dozen sticks until your hands get the hang of it. Then you could move on to less expensive flowers from your local retailer.

Here is a classic, white rose bouquet, perfect for the bride, or, as you will see in subsequent projects, the focal point of any glorious centerpiece. Look for these roses to show up on pages 50 and 54.

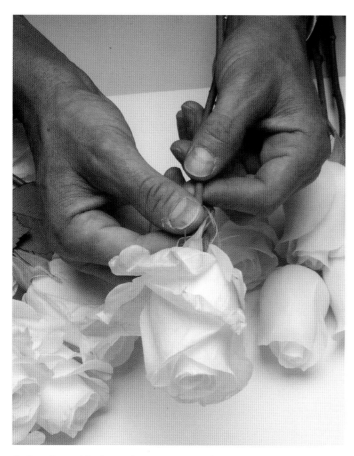

1. Starting with three dozen roses, strip away the leaves and outer guard petals.

2. If the roses have thorns, remove these as well. Use a knife to cut thorns from stems.

3. The first two roses are set to cross one another.

5. The first four roses at right angles.

4. Each time I place a rose they are going on an angle.

6.Place the roses around this center point, rotating and working around the bouquet.

7. This creates a spiral. The bottom should be just as beautiful as the top.

8. While they are loose in your hand, adjust the roses to create a nice crowned effect.

9. Use papered wire to wrap the stems at the tightest gathering point.

10. Finish with a knot. At this point you can add foliage if you want.

11. Using a sprig of Italian ruscus, create a ring by intertwining the stems.

12. Insert the bouquet stems in the ruscus ring. Tie down the ruscus ring with a piece of paper wire.

13. Twist the stems into a solid column and cut the bottoms to a uniform length.

14. A well-constructed bouquet stands on its own. Store it in a vase to keep the flowers fresh. Wrapped like this it can serve as a hand-held bouquet or move it into any floral arrangement.

Harmony Between Bouquet & Vessel

A beautiful bouquet needs a home in which to live. Of course the flowers and their vessel need to complement each other. This book illustrates how important vessels and settings are to the well-constructed, thought-out arrangement.

For starters, I think everyone should own a set of straight vases. You will see these, as well as novelty vessels, throughout this book. This project illustrates the most rudimentary way in which a vase can be dressed up, or down, to provide impact to your floral arrangement.

1. Sticks, wrapped wire, a tall cylinder vase, rubber bands big enough to go around the vase, and some hydrangea team up for an earthy arrangement that is quick and easy to make.

2. Put your rubber bands around the vase.

3. Arrange birch sticks around the container under the rubber band, flush with the base. A curved one like this on the right will mess up the layout and allow gaps. Get rid of this stick. However, if you are wrapping the vase for use with votive candles, maybe you want to create a lot of gaps to allow the light to shine through.

4. After the vase is completely covered in sticks, take paper-wrapped wire and secure with a tight twist at the top and bottom.

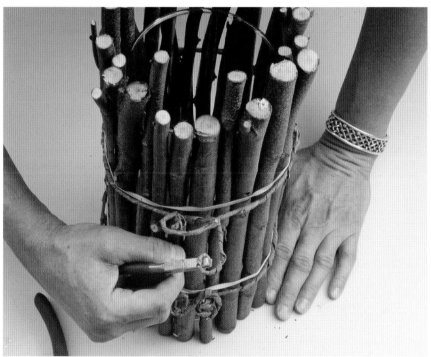

5. Trim the ends of the wires with wire cutters and curl the ends with pliers.

6. The rubber band can be cut off or stretched free for reuse. Ten heads of hydrangea fill the vase for a wonderful show.

Simple Charm

An old-fashioned watering can does not need embellishment. Yet it would be ill paired with a bouquet of expensive white roses. Instead, fresh herbs and flowers from a country garden pair nicely with this vessel and create a delightful centerpiece. In addition to filling the pot with soft greenery, flowering mint sprigs are a great, natural air freshener for the home.

Curly willow gives this arrangement its stature. Keep a bunch of willow on hand— it keeps very well. It is available in craft and florist shops and you can use it fresh, when it is bendable, or you can let it dry.

1. Use an old watering can, some fresh mint, hydrangea, and sunny zinnias for this arrangement.

2. Soak a block of florist foam in warm water and place it in the vessel. Next, add curly willow, followed by sprigs of the blooming mint.

3. Fill the pot with the greenery, the mint, and hydrangea.

4. Then work zinnias or other colorful flowers in amongst the foliage.

Just Picked

Here is an arrangement that appears as though you just stepped in from the garden with an armful of flowers. A simple, old-fashioned tool tray serves as the vessel, and flowers are cleverly arranged to seem like they spill out from one side and the stems from the other.

1. Pink daisies, hypericum, hydrangea, and Italian ruscus are draped in a steel tool tray.

2. Start out with the daisies on one end of the tool box, spraying them out to overhang the box. Save the stems!

3. Work Italian ruscus beneath and between to support the daisies and create a dark backdrop.

4. Place the stems of the daisies coming out the other side, obscured by the ruscus.

5. Intermix a few more daisies with hydrangea blossoms and hypericum berries to add body.

Basket Case

It was a lot of fun to pick some fresh herbs from the garden, snip a few fresh flowers, and carefully arrange them in a basket that looks as though it was casually tipped over. Putting a basket on its side takes the creative impact to a different level, and the mechanics of the process are much simpler than you would expect.

1. We start off with curly willow, purple sage, dahlia, and a small bowl filled with presoaked floral foam.

2. Arrange the willow in the basket.

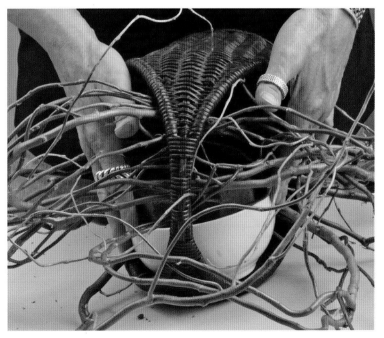

3. Place the basket on its side, but position the bowl upright to support the plants.

19

4. Place the sage first (top left).

5. Because the sage will wilt gracefully in a few days, use some Italian ruscus to help support it and keep the arrangement full (left).

6. Place dahlias and sunflowers randomly in the mix (above).

With pink dahlia and a few sunflowers, this colorful creation has big, charming impact.

A Soda Crate Made Great

Here is another opportunity to take something ordinary and turn it into an arrangement that friends will remember forever. Use it a few times, adding fresh flowers for subsequent occasions, then give it a final makeover and gift it to someone who never had the opportunity to see it on your table.

I painted the soda crate black, which provides a nice background without conflicting colors. You can probably find other crates, baskets, or vessels that can be reinvented with a neutral paint job.

1. Square votives, a painted soda pop crate, flowers, a bird nest with hollow eggs, and a few flowers make a spring display perfect for the casual table.

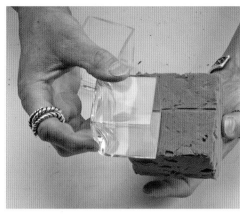

2. Use the votive holder to mark dimensions for the block of floral foam.

3. Cut presoaked floral foam to size.

5. After filling the boxes around the perimeter with an arrangement that pleases you, place your nest in the center.

4. Fill with fresh flowers.

Heirlooms & Nostalgia

Breaking out grandmother's china is an easy way to evoke an instant, nostalgic reaction. To gain impact, pair a few pieces together. I like to work in groupings of threes to play with different heights.

Who says all vases have to be the same? A collection of small and practical family pottery and a mixture of spring flowers, including peonies and hydrangea, create a sentimental centerpiece. Three pieces provide balance and lay out like a triangle.

1. Made for flowers, it is simple to take cuttings from the hydrangea and fill this double trumpet vase. The flowers expand after the bouquet is placed in the vase and allowed to luxuriate in warm water overnight.

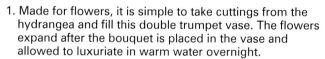

2. Likewise, a mixed bouquet of pink and white peonies is perfect for the single trumpet. Form the heads and leaves into a spiral bouquet (see page 5), trim the stems, and stick them into the vase. I recommend leaving the foliage on the peonies. I think it is almost as pretty as the flower itself.

Another pretty arrangement that plays off the charm of antique pottery and small bunches of floral products with big beauty.

This version features a teapot and two water pitchers filled with roses, hypericum berries, curly willow, and hydrangea.

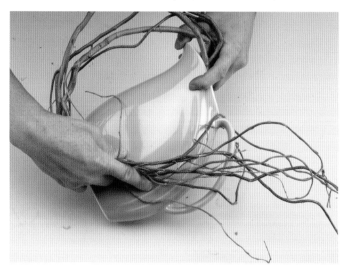

1. Weave the willow through the pitcher opening and handle. Then interweave it with itself to create a halo effect.

2. Roses fill one water pitcher.

3. Hypericum berries make a lovely crown on the small teapot.

Adding Skill & Layers

We are going to start with a basic concept and then explore ways an arrangement can be further ornamented. For this we will use three nesting bowls from the kitchen and a variety of fresh flowers. The purpose of this exercise is to play with the possibilities. What do you have on hand? What is the occasion you are decorating for? Would this look nice done with boxwood and berries for the holidays? The next chapter focuses on impact, be it added drama, or a simple exercise in height and scale.

A set of Fire-King® Jadite bowls will play host to a complementary bouquet of flowers: carnations, cockscomb, daisies, and hydrangea.

1. Cut floral foam to fit each bowl and presoak it. Add the flowers so each species takes up a third of the first layer.

2. Nestle the second bowl on top of the foam in the first bowl and give it a similar treatment as the bowl below. The third bowl nestles on the very top.

The look is more contemporary.

3. Weave lily grass strands in a spiral to create a sense of movement and drama. The ends are carefully inserted through the flowers and into the foam base.

4. Hydrangea wreath.
(see page 104)

Try setting the bowls within the hydrangea wreath (see page 104).

Here the arrangement sits on a pedestal in the hydrangea wreath. Place additional lily grass for height and motion. Sheer, wired ribbon tied into a bow sits atop the centerpiece and cascades down the sides.

Inspiring Awe

The following presentations take your creativity up a notch, illustrating some touches that add awe to a presentation, but are simple to master. Of course, bumping up the scale is part of the next step. As the projects in this chapter progress, you may want to think about getting a bigger table so you can include centerpieces like these in your repertoire!

Appetizing Cluster

Search your cabinets for that seldom used dinnerware. Here is a specialized hors d'oeuvres serving set that we will use to serve something other than food–visual delight!

1. A piece designed to serve four hors d'oeuvres or sauces acts as a wonderful base for a fall arrangement. We start with chrysanthemums, sunflower, willow, roses, and hypericum (left).

2. Presoak floral foam and cut it to fit the cups (center, left).

3. Remove the guard petals from the roses and cut the stems at an angle before inserting them into the foam (center, right).

4. Fill all of the cups in the arrangement (bottom left).

5. Add lily grass for drama (bottom, right).

Fall Splendor

Three nesting copper trays are stacked atop floral foam, and the gaps are filled in with a rainbow of fall flowers. This arrangement could also be set in ice with serving dishes placed amidst the flowers.

1. Celosia, or cockscomb; hypericum; sunflowers; ti leaves; and unique orange roses give this arrangement its autumnal appeal.

2. Pre-soak the foam in warm water and fill the trays with appropriately sized blocks. The foam will not only support the live flowers, but the stacked trays as well. It is important to build a good base with the first tray.

3. When finished, the three trays stack like this.

4. Place the sunflowers first to provide off-center exclamation points throughout the three tiers.

5. Use a knife to cut a small hole in the center of a ti leaf, two-thirds of the way down from the tip. Commonly known as the cast iron plant, ti is a popular houseplant with leaves that are very durable in arrangements.

6. Fill the gaps throughout the arrangement with ti leaf loops. Then punctuate with the bright red cockscomb.

7. Add hypericum.

8. Fill in with roses.

Exotic Overflow

The introduction of an exotic element, in this case dried Brazilian pods, adds intrigue to an enormous display in a big copper kettle. Flowers draw the eye, but relatively few are needed, and the entire arrangement is easily refreshed with a change of greenery. Because the sunflowers have been plucked of their fragile petals, they'll shrink somewhat, but provide eye appeal for weeks. This is a wonderful display to create for your entry hall, where it will provide a whopping first impression.

1. Brazilian pods, curly willow, sunflower, roses, safari sunset leaves, and Italian ruscus complete a fall display.

2. A big copper pot is the heart of this arrangement. Pack it with pre-soaked florist foam. The pot is so large that we use a cardboard box to fill the bottom before we get started.

3. Build a platform by taping together pre-soaked floral foam. Nestle the base in a plastic bag and set it on top of the box.

4. Cut curly willow and insert into the foam base.

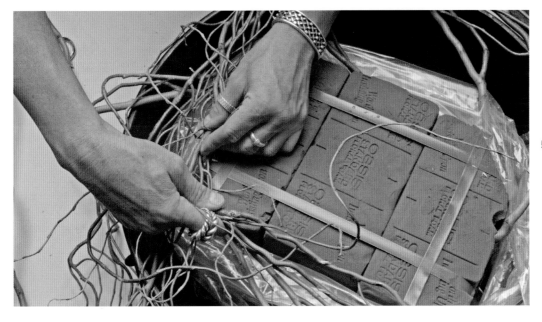

5. Interweave the willow to form a brim around the top of the vessel.

6. Insert galax leaves to cover the plastic liner.

7. Tuck Italian ruscus under the willow to form a new layer.

8. Use safari sunset to form a beautiful inner frame.

9. Position the Brazilian pods and roses on top of the foam bricks.

10. Remove the petals from the sunflowers to create an interesting fall floral effect.

11. Set the newly denuded sunflowers in the Brazilian pods. There is nothing left to wilt on the sunflowers, so you do not need water or foam. Just let them dry.

Evergreen Appeal

Here is another arrangement that will last many weeks. Change the floral elements weekly and water occasionally, and this arrangement will shine through the winter holidays. The orchid's exotic beauty is surprisingly resilient, while the rest of the arrangement will never disappoint.

1. Vines, pine, rattan balls, a copper tray, fresh orchids, and galax leaves pair nicely for a dramatic and earthy holiday display.

2. Place floral foam in the copper tray and top it with Spanish moss to form a base for the arrangement.

3. Arrange two bunches of vines to drape the base.

4. Insert a florist pick in the rattan ball.

Add more rattan balls to the arrangement, placing them in the foam and on the vines.

6. Carefully position an orchid and a bough of pine to support each other and arch over the assembly.

7. Galax leaves obscure the edges and add color.

Going Gaga

Huge pink diamonds are guaranteed to evoke a few squeals of delight at your next celebration. This arrangement is really as simple as investing in an eye shocking vase, and a case of sparkly paste gems. The flowers can vary with the season and the color theme for your event. The assembly takes only moments and you make matching napkin rings a few days in advance (see page 81).

1. Three bunches of pink hydrangeas, four double high-ball glasses, a tall novelty vase, and scads of pink diamond paste gems are the simple ingredients for a centerpiece with big impact.

2. Fill your vase with water before adding the paste gems. This will prevent the glass from shattering when you add the gems. Cut hydrangea stems long enough to reach the water level in the vase. For dramatic effect use a single hydrangea head to fill the novelty vase.

3. Divide another hydrangea into smaller bunches to fill the highball glasses.

Beach Theme

Here is another arrangement that is easily made in advance, quickly refreshed with fresh flowers, and always representative of a popular theme. Shells, some beach grass, and a kaleidoscope of sea glass evoke warm, happy moments.

Shells are easy to find in craft stores, or collect on your own during your next beach vacation. To sterilize them, boil and allow to air dry.

For this arrangement we put our rose bouquet from page 5 to work. There are also ideas for a related napkin ring on page 76.

You can gather and paint your own twigs white to construct the drift fencing, or buy white-washed birch and florist wire at a craft store. At the heart of the arrangement, of course, is the ever-useful straight vase—a critical possession for the creative florist.

1. Components of a beach-
   themed centerpiece: a
   collection of beautiful
   beach glass, shells, and a
   wired "fence" of painted
   sticks, which you can put
   to use in future displays.

2. Cut the painted birch to
   3 or 4 inches long with
   pruning shears.

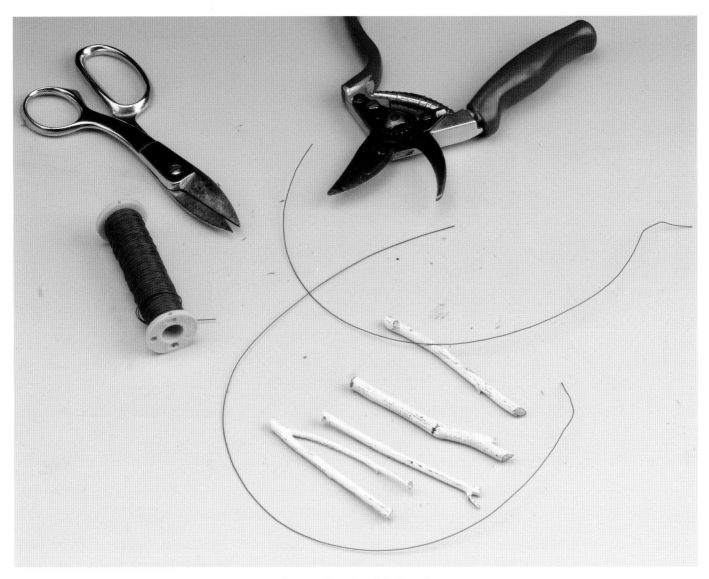

3. Cut two lengths of florist wire.

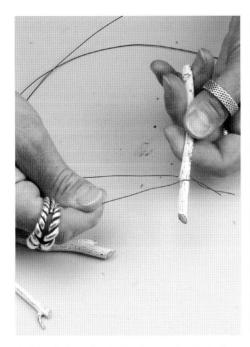

4. Attach the wire to the top of the first stick.

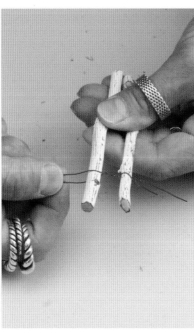

5. Twist several times to create spacing, then insert the next stick.

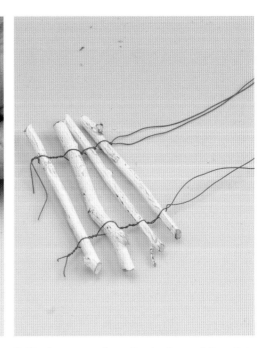

6. Do the same along the bottom of the stick until you have the desired length.

7. Layer sea glass or stones in the base of the vase.

8. Wire the fence together to fit around the vase.

53

9. Arrange the shells around the vase.

10. Finally, add the bouquet.

Towering Delight

By arranging a centerpiece with an airy center and low, grounding focal points, the people who sit around a table are still able to see each other and engage in conversation. A pretty steel frame with crystal pendants supports a frosted glass vase, crowned by our rose bouquet (see page 5). Platforms on the wire frame support three spherical balls festooned with hydrangea. Below, decorative martini glasses support novelty chrysanthemums amidst a bed of rose petals.

Martini Glass Project

Decorating the glasses is great fun and can be done well in advance. Adorned with more or less wire and any variety of flowers, candies, or votive candles, these martini glasses are one of my signature looks. They are never served up solo, but grouped together on tables so they draw attention.

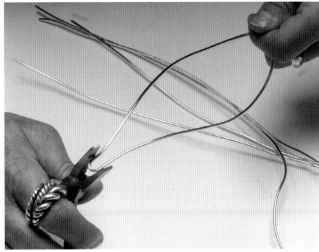

1.Cut a yard of aluminum wire and bend it in half. Use three to six pieces per glass depending on the effect you are aiming for.

2. Use jeweler's pliers to pinch the folded end.

3. Push from the top and middle to create a petal shape.

4. Bend the petal and base wires to fit the shape of the glass.

5. The three petals should fit around the glass like so.

7. Use jeweler's pliers to curl the remaining base wires.

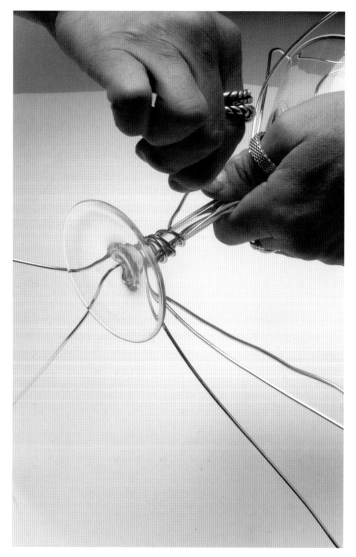

6. Use one of the base wires to wrap the stem and secure the other wires.

The completed wire frame.

Creating a Floral Sphere

Here is an easy project. Our wire frame provides circular platforms perfect for this treatment, but you can use your imagination to find other places to display such floral balls. Set them in candelabra or stick a floral pick through the center and hang them from ribbons.

Cut the stems on some carnations 1 to 2 inches long and insert the flowers into a pre-soaked floral ball. Insert the flowers petal to petal until the sphere is covered. Then place the finished ball on the wire frame.

Romantic Welcome

Here is a lovely entryway adornment. Its heart-shape evokes love and romance. Magnolia and roses paired with fluffy pink hydrangea and mulberry branches crown a basic metal display tray. The magnolia branches rise from the base in a suggestive heart shape, while a path of roses in the pretty, pink background brings in onlookers for a closer look. This spacious centerpiece might also find a home on the buffet or as a delightful focal point in a favorite sitting room.

1. A metal tray, painted black; fresh roses; hydrangea; mulberry branch; and magnolia make this tall, impressive centerpiece.

2. Once the base is prepared with floral foam and Spanish moss, start with the tallest pieces of mulberry branch and magnolia. Coax your arrangement into a form that pleases you.

3. Roses are arranged down the center, like a pathway through bent boughs. These roses are gorgeous, already opened and in their glory. If your roses are still tight, you will need to allow more room for them to expand.

4. Fill in the rest of the base with hydrangea.

5. Adorn the periphery with galax leaves.

Big Bamboo

Every year I teach a class in floral design and this arrangement receives the most "Oohs and Ahhs". It is simple and durable enough that you can use it time and again. Though this bamboo will fade to a tan color, the structures will last forever. The arrangement can be used for candles, flowers, dried arrangements, and so much more. We are using orchids and candles in our bamboo-surrounded vases, and pairing them with fresh orchid napkin rings (see page 101) for an unforgettable table setting. Once again we are using an indispensable set of straight vases.

1. Using bamboo, three sizes of straight vase, binding wire, and decorative rocks, you can create three different configurations with bamboo. Put them all together for a centerpiece. In this section, however, we will only focus on the arrangement on the right. We will need four, 10 inch pieces of bamboo for the uprights, slightly taller than the height of the vase, and eight, 14-inch pieces to run horizontally around the vase.

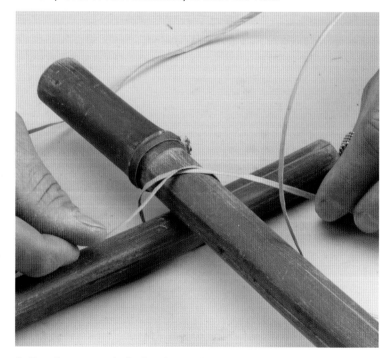

2. Cut about a yard of wire. Start with a knot on top of your first junction, where the base sticks cross at 90-degree angles.

3. Wind in alternate diagonals, finishing with a twist on top.

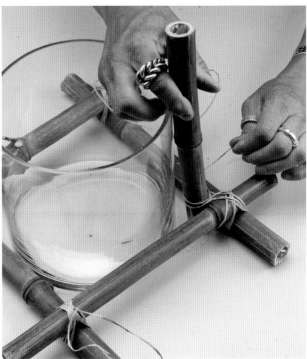

3. Repeat this process in the four corners. Make sure to leave room for the vase in the center.

4. Connect the upright in the corner using the remaining length of wire. Add additional wire if you need it to make the upright secure.

5. After wiring together, attach the second square to the top in the same way.

6. Add a layer of rocks and about 2 inches of water.

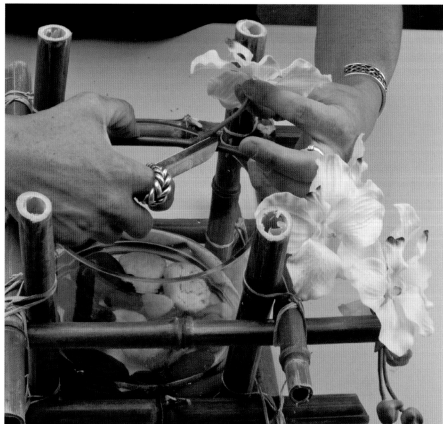

7. Remove individual orchids from the stem and float them on the water. Depending on how fresh the flower was when purchased, they should last in the water for a week or two.

Holiday Bling

I like to use a mixture of ornaments in my holiday decorations to give variety and prevent everything from being exactly the same. I use lots of bulbs to go for a very lush, full centerpiece.

We will form a wonderful table centerpiece using a standard wreath form, a wired pine garland, beaded wire garland, wired silver ribbon, and ornaments in silver and clear.

1. Twist pieces of the wired garland around the frame, working on the back.

3. Then fill in the outer edge of the circle.

2. Work around the center first.

4. Here is the wreath from the back—the entire area is covered. You can mix different garlands for variety, including different sizes.

5. Use standard green florist wire to attach ornaments to the wreath.

6. After all the ornaments are on add the beaded garland, twisting it to the end of the pine garland.

7. Add the wired ribbon with the same technique, twisting the pine garland to the branches to secure it. Just let it dance across the wreath without creating any particular pattern to give the piece a sense of movement. Roll the ends into a swirl, using several lengths of ribbon to create a number of these rolls that will lie on the wreath.

8. The finished wreath bursts with random magic.

9. Nestle a pedestal base in the middle to support a candle, and add more wire bead garland. You can also fill this with fruit or fresh flowers.

Finishing the Table

Marrying the centerpiece with other elements on the table is important and fun! Napkin rings are a simple approach to tying the place setting to your event's theme.

Charged with Impressing

For the more elaborate affair, a special charger plate (the plate that holds the diner's place until the first course arrives) is another opportunity to ply your creativity.

Decorative charger: a placeholder removed after the first course arrives. A small dish could be placed on this with hors d'oeuvres.

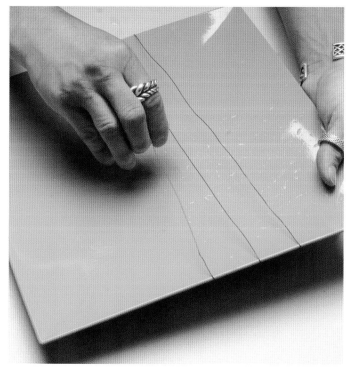

1. Wire, assorted beads, galax leaves, daisies, and florist foam adorn this decorative, square plate, which can then act as a centerpiece or, made in bulk, place savers for each place setting (top).

2. Cut a small cube from the foam and presoak in warm water. Use a knife to round off the edges. This gives you more surface area to work with when you are inserting flowers (above).

3. Wrap the plate with wire three times in one direction (right).

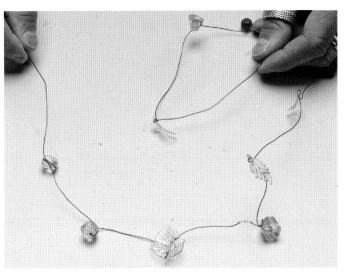

5. Cut a length of wire about a yard long. Add beads and then twist into place every 2 to 4 inches.

4. Use the same or alternate color to wrap the plate twice in the other direction.

6. Use the beaded length of wire to secure the foam-based oasis on the plate.

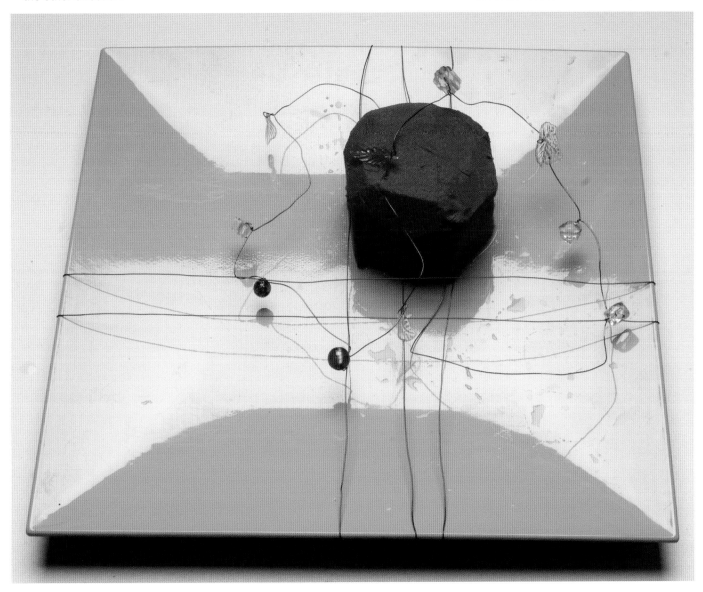

7. Add just enough galax leaves to cover the foam. Usually one bunch is sufficient.

8. Place daisies in the center.

9. Place hypericum berries to fill the arrangement. Then insert fronds of lily grass at the base, arch the grass over the arrangement, and tuck it under the wires that wrap the plate.

10. Use a short length of wire shaped into a "U" to secure he arch of grass to the front side of the arrangement.

Just Beachy

Designed to pair with the centerpiece arrangement on page 50, this fun, shell-encrusted wire ring is sturdy enough to reuse. This procedure is a sure fix for those with the urge to craft.

1. Start with a smartly striped, beachy napkin; whitewashed birch (sold in craft stores); some florist wire; a few pretty shells; and a little beach grass. Refer to page 51 to get started with your wired "fence."

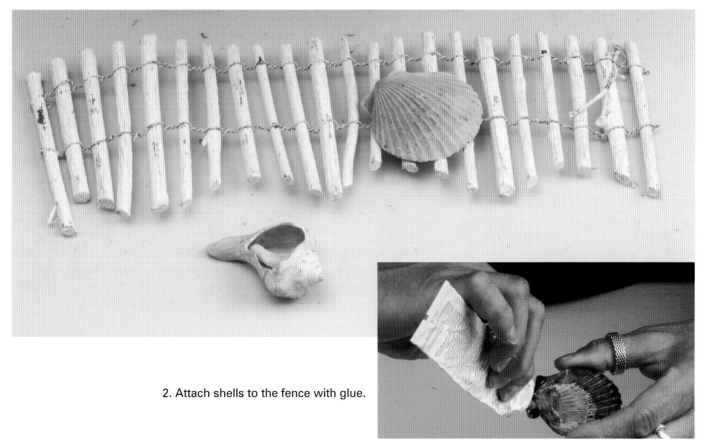

2. Attach shells to the fence with glue.

3. Fold the napkin in half to create a triangle.

4. Fold the bottom corners to the top.

5. Turn the folded napkin over.

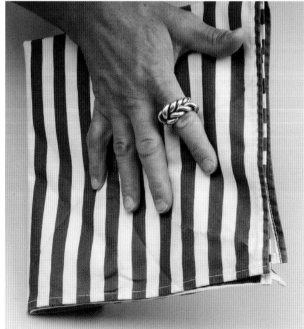

6. Fold the corners into the center.

8. Turn the napkin over again.

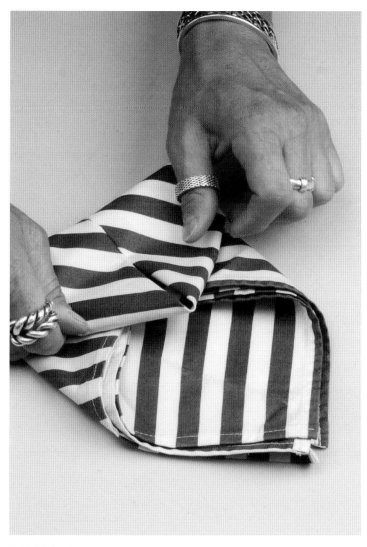

7. Fold the bottom up.

9. Slip the napkin into the napkin ring.

9. Fold the corners of the napkin back.

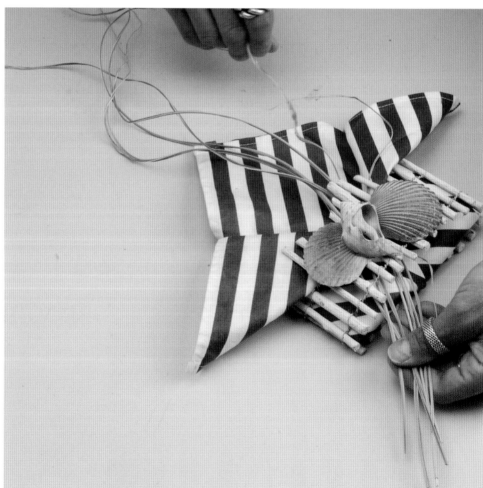

10. Insert the dried grasses.

A Gem of a Setting

Diamonds are a girl's best friend, so they say, but pink shiny paste gems can also excite a crowd. Try pairing this pretty napkin ring with some flowers, placing the fan-like creations on a table centered around the arrangement on page 48. The entire arrangement is easily completed, but will not be easily forgotten.

1. Create magic with pretty, pink alstroemeria; diamond-shaped paste gems; and simple florist wire.

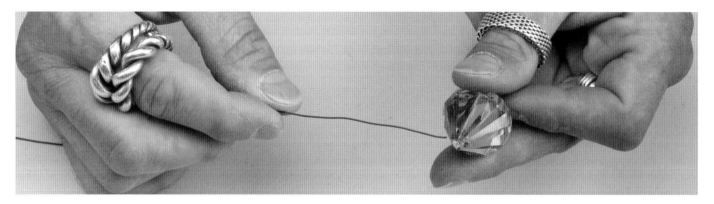

2. String the paste gems on the florist wire.

3. Make the string long enough to form a napkin ring.

4. Twist the wires together and trim the ends.

5. Fold the napkin in half, then begin an accordion fold.

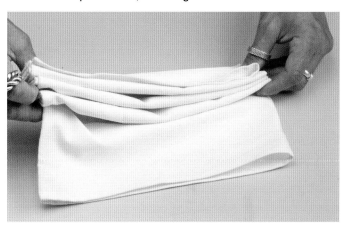

6. Continue folding over and under.

8. Insert the folded end into the gem ring. Add fresh flowers just before the event gets underway.

7. Fold the bottom of the accordion.

Message in a Bottle

You can use this delightful bottle-centered napkin ring many times over. Fit with fresh flowers, or perhaps a mysterious message, prior to each event. Use wire to match your martini-glass centerpieces (page 56), or flowers that complement your floral display, tying your table together.

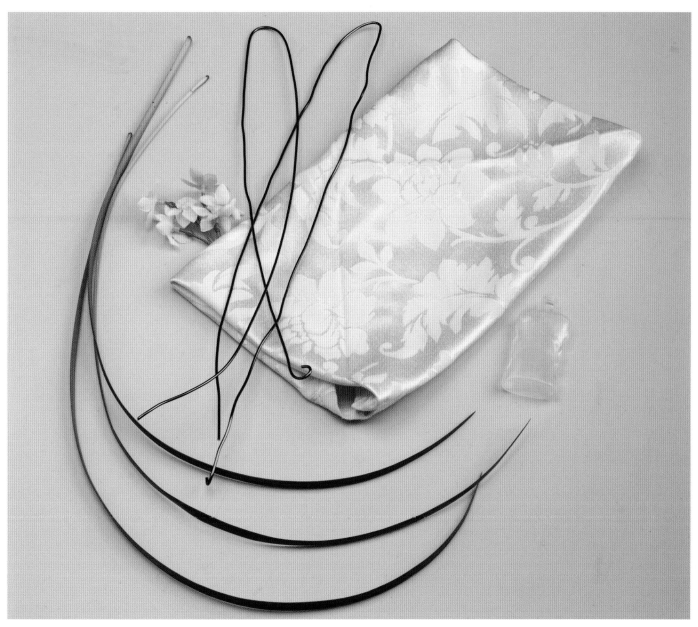

1. A textured, satin napkin; fresh daffodils; lily grass; and a decorative bottle team up on a wire structure for a great napkin setting.

2. Fold the corners of the napkin into the center.

3. Roll it up and flatten it.

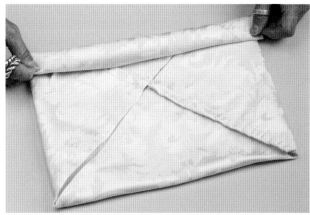

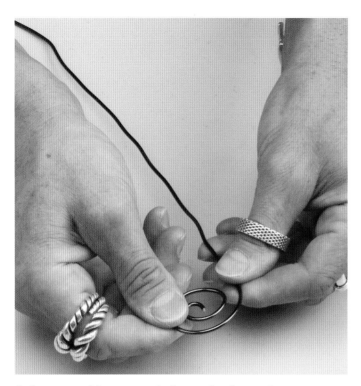

4. Create a swirl at one end of your aluminum wire.

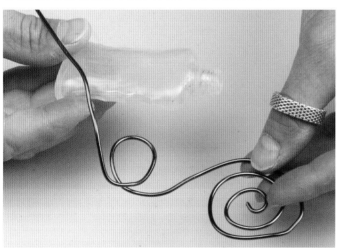

5. Fashion a base where the bottle will rest.

7. Finish with another swirl at the end of the wire, leaving room for a loop that will encircle the napkin.

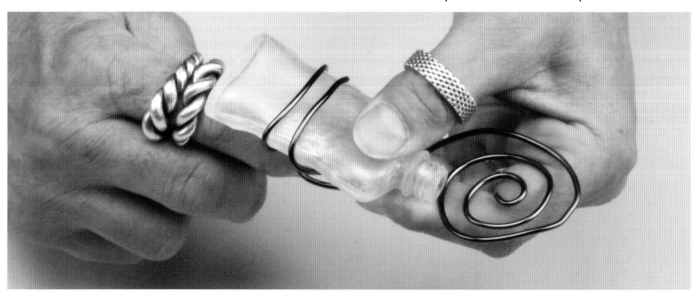

6. Wrap the bottle with wire.

86

8. Attach the napkin to the final structure, which you can do weeks ahead of the event. Add the fresh flower and grass just before the event.

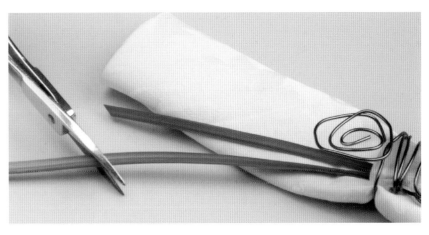

9. Feed lily grass under and through the wire and trim to fit.

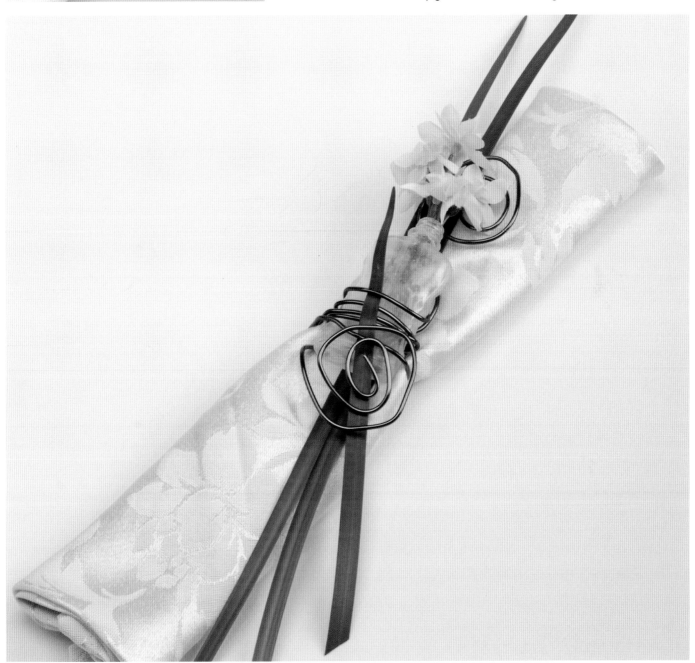

10. The stems of small flowers simply pop into the bottle.

Sparkling Setting

Decorative aluminum wire and beaded wire are two of my favorite tools for creating fabulous effects. They truly make your work shine, but also connect items to form frameworks upon which you can build.

Here is a way to let your creative side cut loose—use any kind of flower and any color bead and wire to suit your occasion.

1. Fold the napkin into a square (quartered).

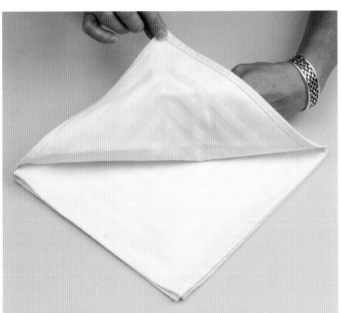

2. Fold back the top quarter to form a triangle.

3. Fold back the next layer partway and tuck it under.

4. Flip the napkin to the other side.

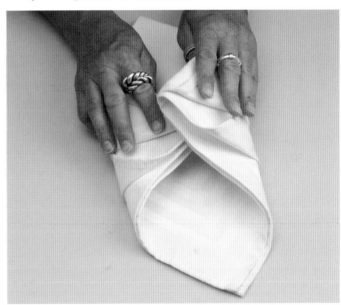

5. Fold the corners to the center.

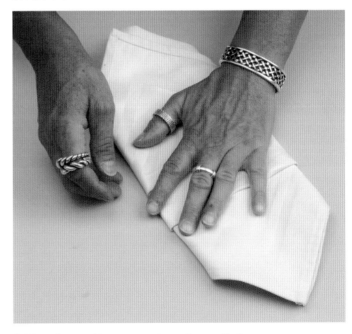

6. Turn the napkin over again and smooth it.

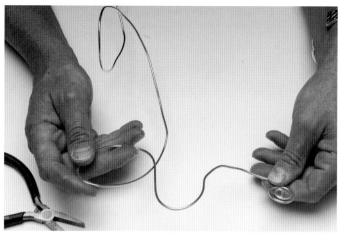

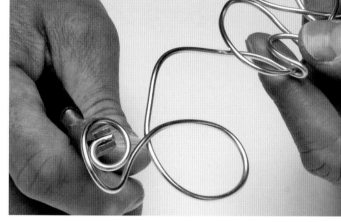

7. Starting with 12 gauge aluminum wire, form a swirl at the end.

9. Create a swirl at the terminus. This is how I do all my clasps because they work so well and are easy to adjust for different size napkins.

8. Create a free-form wire base about 10 inches long, folding and overlapping.

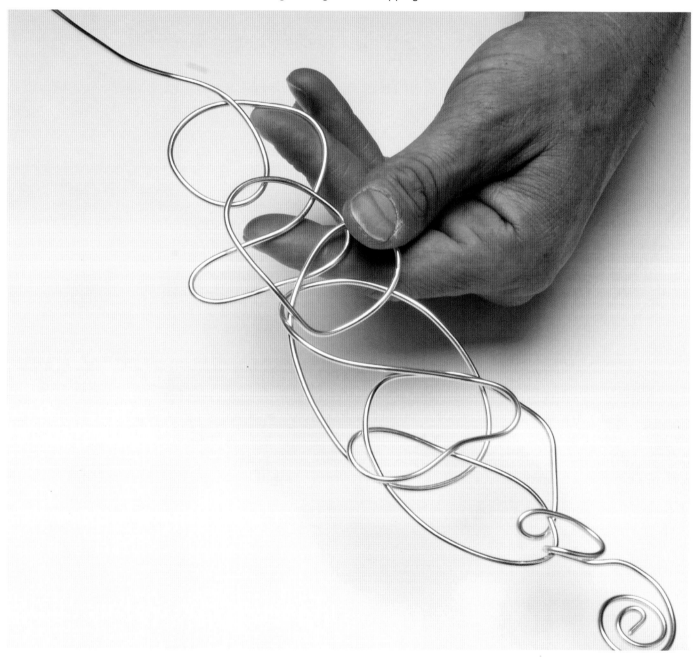

10. Use about a yard of beaded garland, which is available in most craft stores.

11. Wrap the free-form base with the garland, lending strength to the construction.

13. Cut cockscomb into small pieces. I love this flower because it comes apart so easily and creates interesting shapes.

12. Bend the pieces up so the beads will spray away from the napkin, but leave a flat side that will go around the napkin.

14. Apply floral glue to the back of a floret and attach it to the wire form.

15. After the glue sets, bend the form into a ring.

16. Slip the napkin into place.

17. Fold back the point of the napkin.

Daisy Ring

This project takes the wire napkin ring base up a notch, creating a more formal base to use and reuse as a napkin ring. In this case, we have decked it with daisies for irresistible, casual charm.

We will be creating a basic form that you can use time and time again for napkin rings, or even as a fresh flower bracelet. If you look closely, you can see the dried bases of flowers that previously graced this form. Fresh ones can be glued right over top.

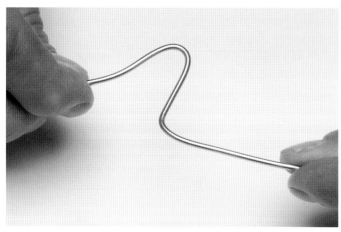

1. Using 12 gauge aluminum wire, create a "Z"-shaped kink 3 or 4 inches from the end of the wire.

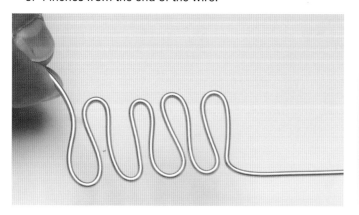

2. Start creating a zigzag formation, bending it by hand. The zigzag length will be 5 to 6 inches long.

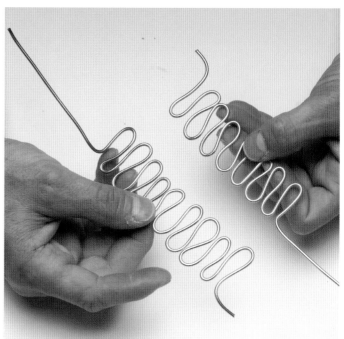

3. When it is long enough, cut near the last zigzag and make a matching piece with the same height and length.

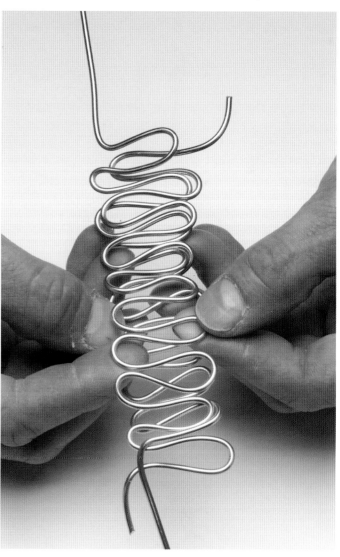

4. With the two long ends extending out either side, blend the two pieces together, interweaving the loops.

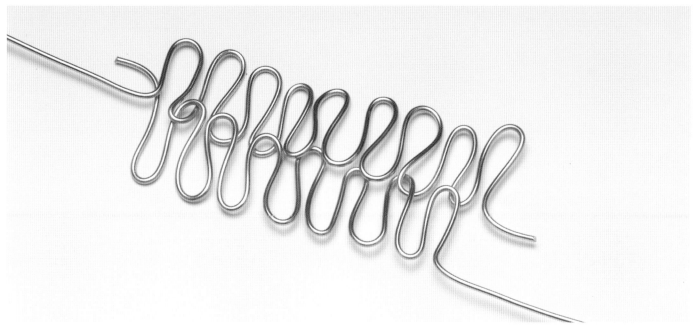

5. The pieces are now connected.

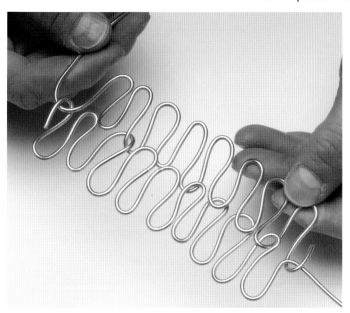

6. Interlock the ends, closing the short end around the long one to lock it in place.

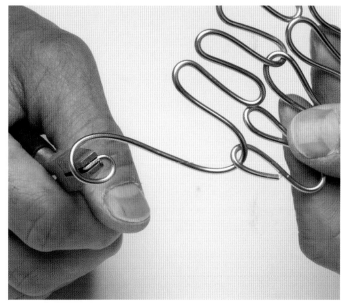

7. Using flat jewelry pliers, make a swirl with the longer ends on either side.

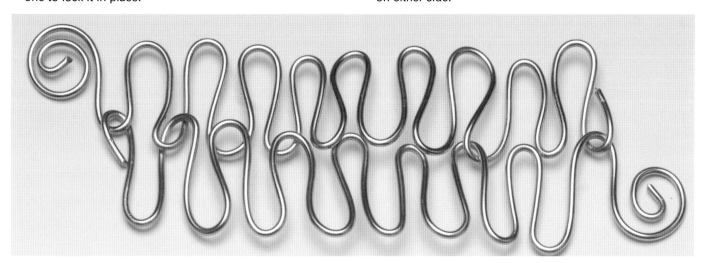

8. The basic form is finished.

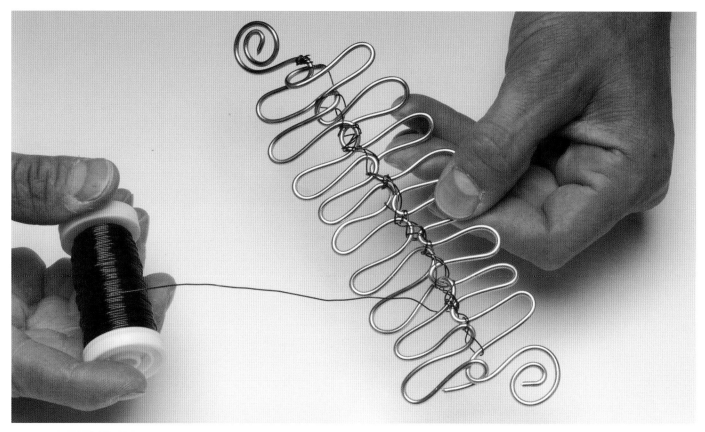

9. Using a finer wire (a 28 gauge wire will do), wrap the two pieces and lock them together.

10. Remove flowers from stems—it could be any kind of flower. Using Oasis floral adhesive for fresh flowers, apply to both the base of the flower and a good connection spot on the bracelet.

11. After the flowers are applied, attach Italian ruscus leaves with glue as accents.

12. After the glue sets connect the ends of the ring.

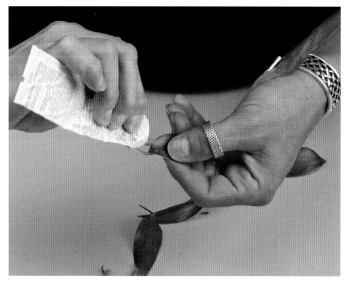

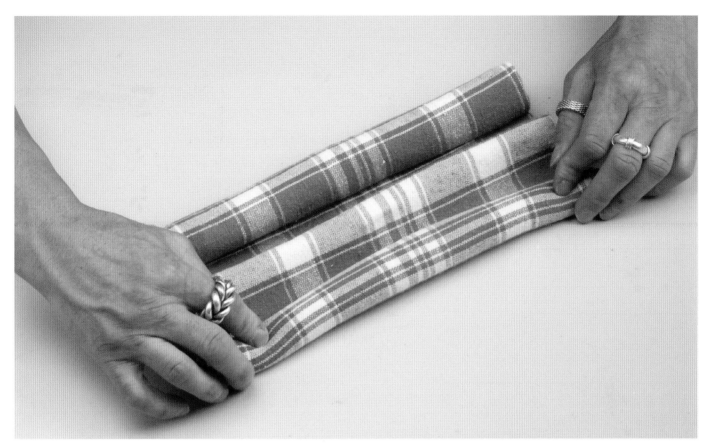

13. Fold the napkin in half then roll it toward the center from either side.

14. Leave a hump in the center.

15. Insert the napkin through the ring.

Holiday Setting

Pine boughs evoke a country Christmas in a simple construction tied together with inexpensive twine.

Some fresh pine, twine, a napkin, and a plate are the components of a Christmas place setting.

1. Roll both sides of the napkin together to the center.

2. Fold the bottom third up.

3. Cut two, 30 inch lengths of twine.

4. Fold the two lengths of twine in half and place them on top of each other to form a right angle.

5. Interlock the doubled pieces and fold.

6. Knot the ends together.

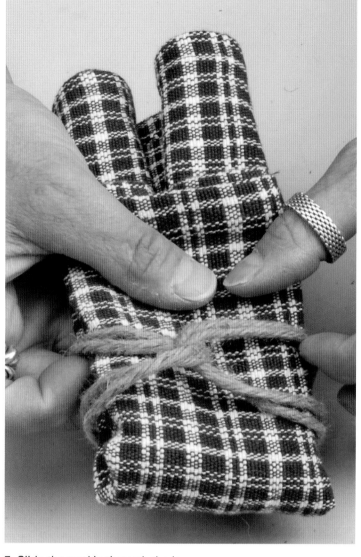

7. Slide the napkin through the loop.

8. Insert the pine bough and arrange.

Bamboo Two

Here we revisit our bamboo table setting (page 63), constructing the napkin rings that complement the look so perfectly (*below left*). The secret is equisetum, a grass available in most craft and floral shops that recreates the look of bamboo on a smaller scale. It is easy to cut with scissors and dries nicely, so your work will be preserved.

1. Equisetum, a grass that looks like bamboo, and a little bit of fresh orchids connected with glue make matching napkin rings.

2. Cut the equisetum to 6 inch pieces. You will need eight pieces per napkin ring.

4. Attach the glued joints to the top and bottom pairs, creating a frame.

3. Line up the eight lengths, then apply glue to the joints at the top and bottom of the pieces, where the pairs will cross.

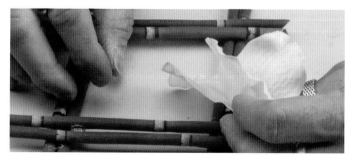

5. Use floral glue to affix a fresh flower to one corner. Later, when the event is over and the flower has wilted, you can remove the flower and use the frame for a picture, or your next dinner party!

Hang it All

We have embellished all the horizontal surfaces, so now we will take to the air to contemplate other spaces to place arrangements. Wreaths are a wonderful way to create a vertical adornment for your home, though they also lay quite nicely on a tabletop—alone or as a frame for your arrangements. You might also want to raise your centerpiece above the table, as you will see with an embellished chandelier.

A wire floral wreath is the easiest way to create an enduring wall hanging. For more temporary, living floral displays, you will want to start with a moist ring of florist foam. The chandelier project, however, has a mix of fresh flowers and silk flowers, and can be rejuvenated around the calendar to reflect the season or the theme of your event. These arrangements will carry you from the New Year all the way through to the next holiday season.

Basic Wreath Construction

This snowball hydrangea, picked at its summer peak, will dry and remain exactly like this forever. I like to make these in the summer, then spray paint them silver or gold for Christmas. A pretty wreath can decorate your table or greet guests at the door. You can use the same technique with bundles of pine, eucalyptus, or lavender.

You will need florist wire, fresh hydrangea, and a standard wire wreath frame.

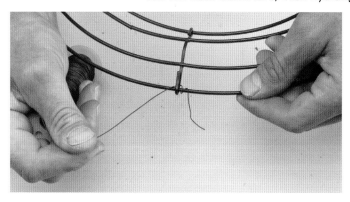

1. Attach the end of the wire to the frame.

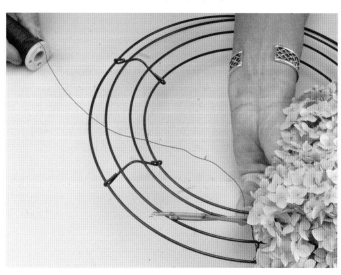

2. I always add a pair of hydrangea bunches together. Lay them on the frame with stems together and then wrap wire around about three times to make sure it is secure.

3. Lay successive pairs over each other and wire in place. It is important to make little bundles and tie them fast. Otherwise the flowers will fall off when you pick the wreath up.

4. The final bunch is squeezed in and wired into place.

5. After securing the final bunch, cut and secure the wire on the back.

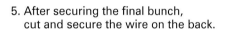

6. Remove any stems that poke out.

Topping It Of

For our final arrangement we will create a dramatic chandelier using fresh and silk flowers that can be easily updated throughout the year. If you are concerned with the fire hazard of using traditional candles in this arrangement, you can substitute battery powered acolyte candles.

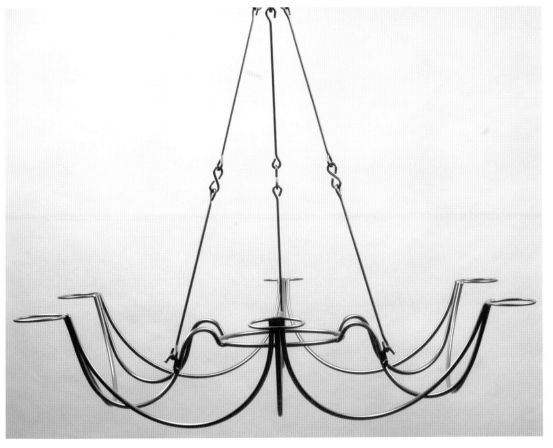

1. A basic chandelier frame serves as our easel.

2. Slip a large wreath form bejeweled in beaded wire onto the chandelier form.

107

3. Fluff the beaded wire to stand out dramatically from the frame.

4. Add weeping pussy willow, weaving it into the framework of the wreath. The vines interweave over the wreath form and up the candelabra support.

5. Add silk passionflower. Real passion flowers only last one day.

6. Add a vase filled with water to the center ring.

7. Drop a spiral bouquet of stock, constructed just like the rose bouquet (see page 5), into the center.

8. Finally, add candles to the candelabra. Because of fire regulations in many places, battery operated acolyte candles have become popular.

About the Author

Bill Murphy, AIFD, CFD, got his start in York, Pennsylvania. He studied art at Antonelli Institute of Art and Photography (now the Art Institute of York, PA) and launched his professional career as an interior designer. However, response to his hobby of floral design led to a new career. In addition to private events, he is a designer creating showroom displays throughout the United States. His work has been featured in The Knot, Floral Design, Modern Bride, and many regional publications. He is a presenter at the coveted National Symposium of the American Institute of Floral Design. More of his work can be seen at www.cuttingedgefloral.com.

Supply List

The greenery used throughout the book may vary in your local market and by season. Check with your local florist for availability. Also, the vessels and other non-organic decorations used throughout were chosen because they are more than likely readily available. Sourcing these items in creative and resourceful ways before starting is part of the fun and artistry of making floral centerpieces.

There are, however, many supplies used throughout this book that you should make sure you have before getting started. These items should be available at your local craft store.

NOTE: Most of the items used in this book come from Oasis Floral Products in Kent, Ohio. For more information, please contact 1-800-321-8286 or http://sona.oasisfloral.com.

- aluminum wire (12 gauge and 28 gauge)
- battery powered acolyte candles
- beaded wire
- beads
- cardboard boxes
- colored wires
- faux gems (paste gems)
- floral foam
- floral glue
- florist pick
- florist wire
- jeweler's pliers
- knife
- papered wire
- plastic bag
- pruning shears
- ribbon
- rubber bands
- scissors
- seashells and sea glass
- twine
- wire cutters
- wire wreath frame
- wired ribbon